POWER SYSTEM ENGINEERING DIPLOMA & ENGINEERING MCQ

MANOJ DOLE

Contents

Foreword

Power System Engineering Diploma & Engineering MCQ is a simple Book for Power System Diploma & Engineering Course, It contains objective questions with underlined & bold correct answers MCQ covering all topics including all about the latest & Important about Fluid Mechanics, Thermodynamics, Mechanics of Deformable Bodies , Circuit Theory & Network, Electrical Electronic Measurement, Fluid Machinery, Engineering Thermodynamics, Materials Science and Technology, Theory of Machines, Electrical Machines, Digital Electronics & Integrated Circuits, Renewable Energy Systems, Hydro Power Generation, Nuclear Power Generation, Electrical Machines, Heat Transfer, Microprocessor and Microcontrollers, Steam Generators and its Auxiliaries, Steam Turbines and its Auxiliaries, Electrical Equipment in Power Station, Power Transmission and Distribution, Control Systems, Refrigeration and Air Conditioning, High Voltage Engg. and lots more.

We add new question answers with each new version. Please email us in case of any errors/omissions. This is arguably the largest and best Book for All engineering multiple choice questions and answers.

As a student you can use it for your exam prep. This Book is also useful for professors to refresh material.

Preface

This book may be purchased for educational, business, or sales promotional use. Online edition is also available for this title. For more information, contact our corporate/institutional sales department: [+919921582799] or [manojdole1@gmail.com]

While every precaution has been taken in the preparation of this book, the publisher and authors assume no responsibility for errors or omissions, or for damages resulting from the use of the information contained herein.

About the Author

MANOJ DOLE is an Engineer from reputed University. He is currently working with Government Industrial Training- Institute as a lecturer from last 12 Years. His interest include- Engineering Training Material, Invention & Engineering Practical- Knowledge etc.

CHAPTER ONE

Power System Engineering Hand Tools & Measuring Instruments Theory

Download App   Online Test Exam   ITI Books   AutoCAD CAM   JOB & Apprentice

Online Theory   Computer Course   Trading Course   CNC Course   MSCIT Course

Shopping Business   Internet Business   Web Designing   Online Services   Top Sportsmans

Indian Army   Freedom Fighters   Top Scientists   Social Reformers   Motivational Speaker

Top Richest People   Join WhatsApp Group   Join Facebook Group   Like Facebook Page   PAN / Adhar / Licence Passport

Fire extinguisher

Calliper

Hacksaw frame

Universal surface guage

Hammer

Centre punch

Bench vice

Files

Scraper

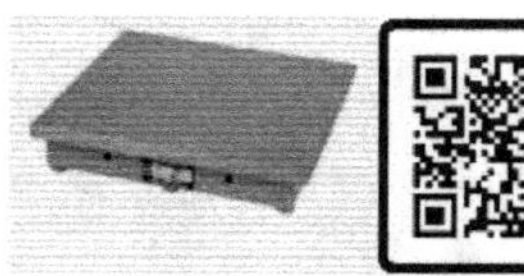

Surface Plate

Outside Micrometer

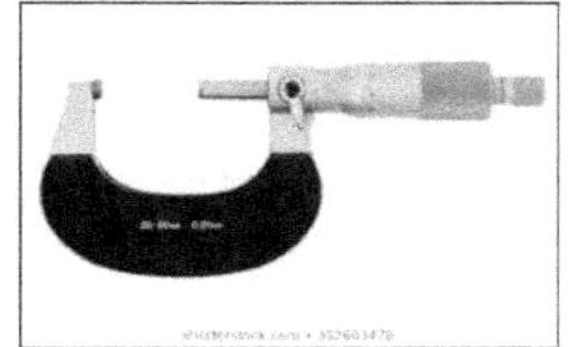 

Micrometer

Depth micrometer

Vernier Calliper

Vernier bevel protractor

Drilling

Reamer

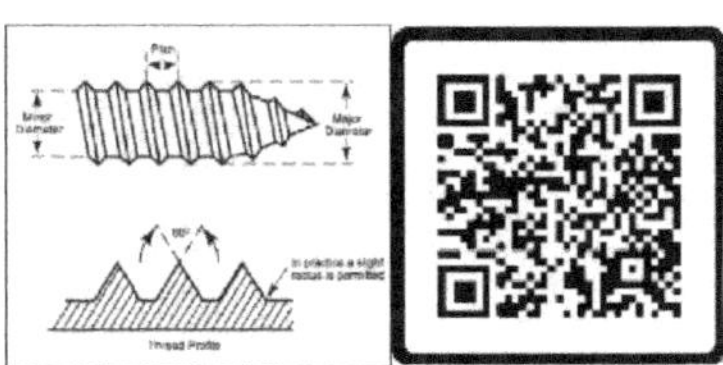

Thread

Tap Die

Grinding Wheel

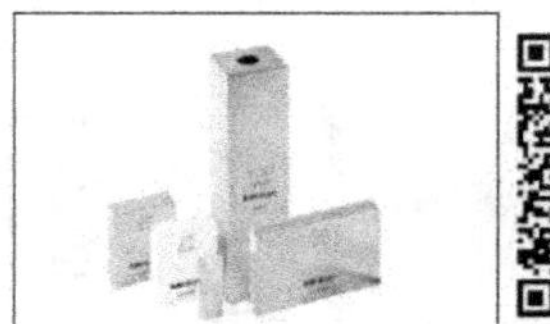

Slip gauge

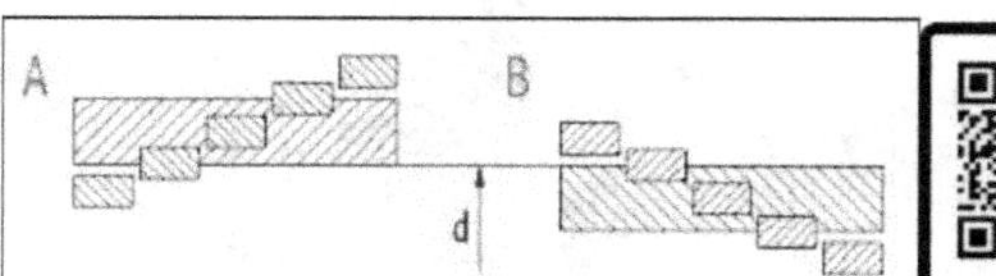

Limit fit tolerance

Lathe Machine

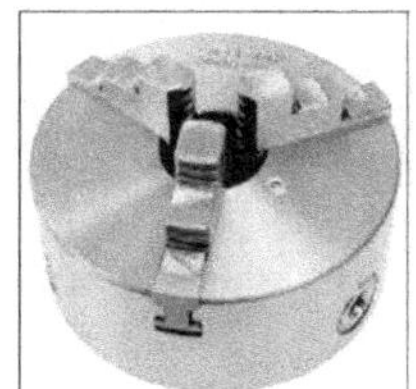

Lathe chuck

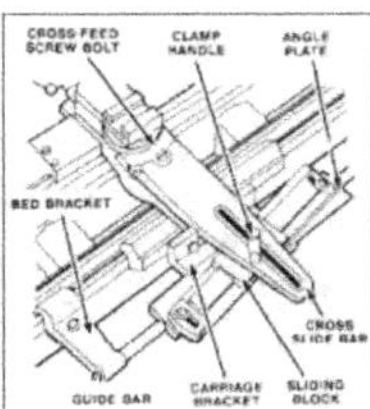

Taper turning attachment

taper ring gauge

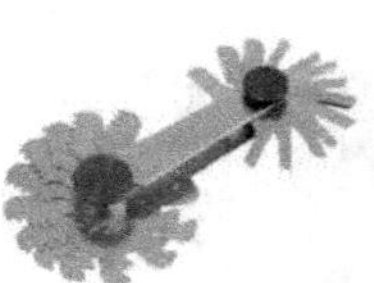 

screw pitch gauge

Gear

screw pitch gauge

Tap Die

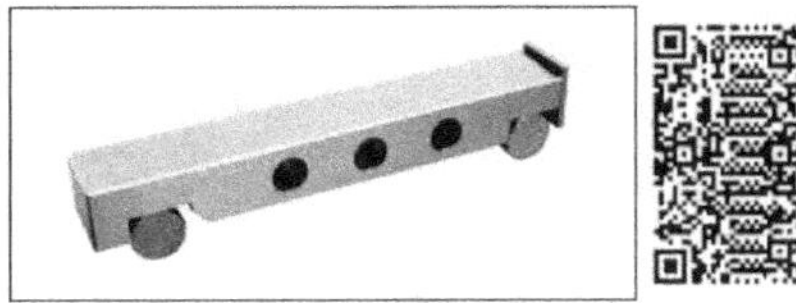

Sine bar

Slip gauge

Dial test indicator

Telescopic gauge

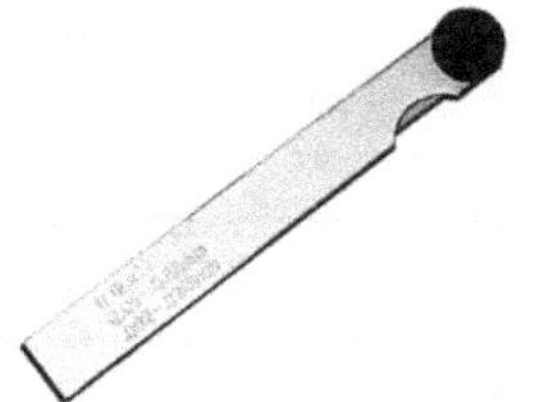

Feeler gauge

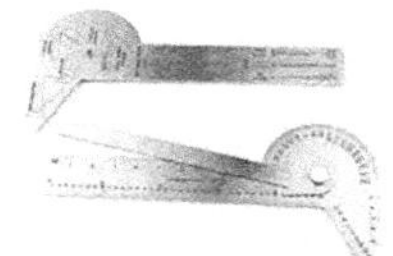

Centre gauge

Jig

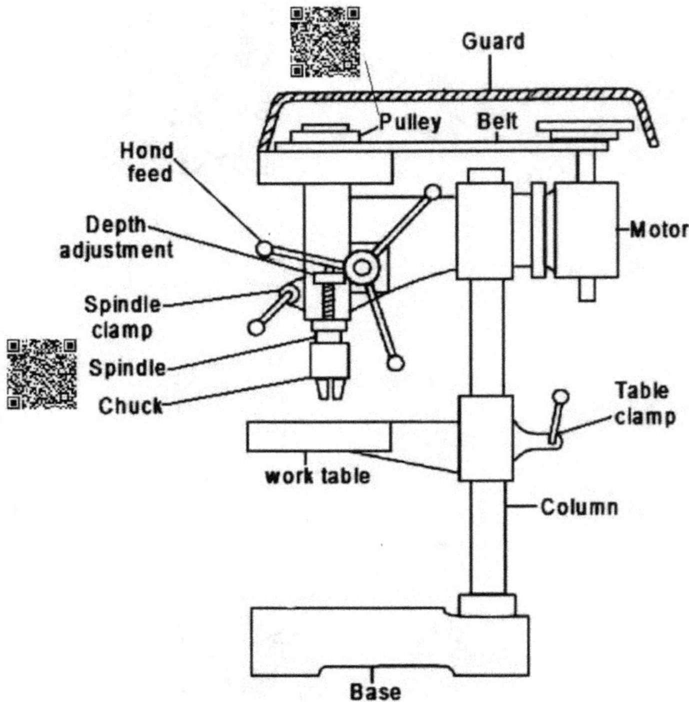

Piller Drilling Machine

CHAPTER TWO

Power System Engineering MCQ

Safety Precaution in Power System Engineering

01] In case of bleeding, take treatment Of

<u>A] spray cold water</u>

B] Bandage immediately -----]

C] Enquire about the accident thought treatment

D] cold 3" and rest

02] in case of an accident, the victim should im

A] Asked to take rest

<u>C] Attended immediately</u>

D] leave him

03] First aid is given to an injured or ill person primarily....

A] Save life

B] Prevent further deterioration of the muff's

C] Give best possible comfort

<u>D] All of these</u>

04] Colour code for Bins for waste paper segregation is -----

<u>A] blue Colour</u>

B] Yellow Colour

C] Red Colour

D] Green Colour

05] In Japanese Seiko stands for --------------

<u>A] Shine</u>

B] Sort

C] Standardize

D] Sustain

06] Benefit of SS system is ------

A] Increase in productivity

B] Increase in quality

C] Reduction in wastage of time

D] All of these

07] Safety is -----------

A] nobody's business

B] every bodise business

C] Some bodies business

D] The organization business

08] For basic categories of safety signs are available The meaning of"prohibition" sign ----

A] shows it must not be done

B] Shows what must be done

C] Warns the hazard or danger

D] Gives information of safety provision

09] Which one is a workshop safety?

A] Keep shop floor clean and free from grease, oil or other slippery materials

B] Stop the machine before changing the speed

C] Don't use cracked or chipped tools

D] Don't try to stop a running machine with hand

10] In Personal Protect Equipment (PPE] HELMET is used to

A] protect head

B] Protect eyes

C] Protect hands

D] Protect ears

11] Which of the following belongs to general safety?

A Have a worker in good attitude

B] The work clean and clear

C] Concentrate on your work

D] Keep the floor and gangways clean and clear

12] While grinding, which is used to protect the eyes?

A] Dark green glass

B] Mask

C] Sun glasses

D] Safety goggles

13] Which of the following is done for machine safety?

A] Check the oil level before starting the machine

B] Do things in a methodical way

C] Keep the floor and gangways clean and clear

D] Don't use dies and scarves

14] In Personal Protect Equipment (PPE], 'sleeves' is used to protect ----------

A] Face

B] Eyes

C] Ears

D] Hands

15] ABC stands for --------------

A] Automatic Breathing Control

B] Automatic Blood Control

C] Airway Breathing Circulation

D] Automatic Blood Circulation

16] To put off"Class B" fire, the types of fire extinguisher used is ....]

A] dry power

B] Carbon dioxide

C] Jet of water

D] Foam type

17] Which type of fire extinguisher is used to put off general fire?

A] Water type Extinguisher

B] Foam type Extinguisher

C] Dry chemical powder Extinguisher

D] Carbon dioxide (C02] Extinguisher

Hand Tools in Power System Engineering

18] One micrometer (U] is equal to...

A] 0.1mm

B] 0.01mm

C] 0.001mm

D] 0.0001mm

19] Name the tool used to make and finish the leak proof joints of a pipe T joint

A] groover

B] setting hammer

C] creasing hammer

D] round bottom stake

20] Portion of the hammer used for fixing the handle is...

A] Face

B] Peen

C] Cheek

D] <u>Eye hole</u>

21] Weight of the hammer for the marking purpose is...

A] <u>250g</u>

B] 500g

C] 1 kg

D] 2 kgs

22] To cut out small apertures which punch and die type of machine is used?

A] shear type nibbler

B] <u>punch type nibbler</u>

C] circular cutting machine

D] guillotine shearing machine

23] Scribers are made of...

A] Mild steel

B] <u>High carbon steel</u>

C] Brass

D] Cast iron

24] The size of an engineer's vice is specified by the...

A] Length of the movable jaw

B] <u>Width of the jaws</u>

C] Height of the vice

D] Maximum opening of the jaws

vice   Bench vice

Bench Vice

25] The form of thread used in carpenters vice is...

A] Square

B] Acme thread

C] <u>Sawtooth Thread</u>

D] Knuckle thread

26] The convexity of files helps...

A] To file concave surfaces

B] To file convex surfaces

C] <u>To prevent rounding of edges of work</u>

D] The file to become straight when pressure is applied

27]] Name the instrument used to check the perpendicularity of the branch pipe with the main pipe of a pipe T joint

A] protractor

B] <u>try square</u>

C] spirit level

D] straight edge

28] The caliper meant for measuring the width of a slot is...

A] Odd leg caliper

B] Outside caliper

C] Jenny caliper

D] <u>Inside calliper</u>

29] The included angle of the groove of 'V' block is always....

A] 45°

B] 60°

C] 90°

D] <u>120°</u>

<u>v blocks</u>

<u>v block</u>

'V' blocks

30] 'V' blocks are available in grades of...
A] <u>A & B</u>
B] A,B & C
C] 1,2 & 3
D] 1 & 2
31] 'V' blocks of grade 'B' are made of
A] <u>Cast iron</u>
B] Mild steel
C] Steel
D] Cast steel
32] 'V' block 50/5-40 A is used for holding jobs of diameter
A] Ø 50 mm
B] Ø 5 to Ø 50 mm
C] <u>Ø 5 to Ø 40 mm</u>
D] Ø 40 mm
33] The reason for using cast iron in making 'V' blocks
A] to increase the weight of the block

B] to reduce the cost

C] <u>to reduce the friction</u>

D] to get a good appearance

34] For cutting thin tubing, the most suitable pitch of the hacksaw blade is...

A] 1.8mm

B] 1.4mm

C] 1mm

D] <u>0.8mm</u>

35] For cutting solid brass, the most suitable pitch of the hacksaw blade is...

A] <u>1.8mm</u>

B] 1.4mm

C] 1mm

D] 0.8mm

36] A new hacksaw blade after a few strokes becomes loose because of the...

A] <u>Stretching of the blade</u>

B] Wing-nut threads being worn out

C] Wrong pitch of the blade

D] Improper selection of the set of saws.

37] While cutting small diameter pipes, it is advisable to watch regularly and ensure that...

A] The cut is along the curved line

B] <u>More saw teeth are in contract</u>

C] The work is not overheated

D] Proper balancing of hacksaw is maintained

Drilling in Power System Engineering

38] If the drill runs untrue, it will

A] get too hot

B] cut undersize

C] distort the spindle

D] <u>cut an oversized hole</u>

39] Running the drill too fast many result in

A] <u>spoiling the cutting edge</u>

B] poor surface finish

C] twisting the tang

D] drilling an oval hole

40] A drill with worn land will

A] drill hole oversize

B] <u>drill hole undersize</u>

C] run out of centre

D] drill an accurate hole

41] The morse taper provided on drills used on lathe ranges between

A] <u>MT1 to MT5</u>

B] MT1 to MT4

C] MT0 to MT5

D] MT0 to MT4

42] Feeding the small drill too fast into the work may result in

A] <u>breaking the drill</u>

B] bending the drill

C] cutting an oval shape hole

D] increased production

43] The drill size for a M 20 tap is

A] <u>17.5 mm</u>

B] 18 mm

C] 18.5 mm

D] 19 mm

44] The taper shank drills are held on the machine by means of...

A] Chucks

B] <u>Sleeves</u>

C] Drift

D] Vice

45] Drill chucks are fitted on the drilling machine spindle by means of a...

A] Knurled ring

B] <u>Arbor</u>

C] Drift

D] Pinion and key

drill chuck

drilling

Drill Chuck

46] The Morse taper provided on drills ranges between...

A] <u>MT 1 to MT 5</u>

B] MT 1 to MT 4

C] MT 0 to MT 5

D] MT 0 to MT 4

47] A drift is used for...

A] Drawing a drill location

B] Fixing chuck on the machine spindle

C] Removing a broken drill from the work

D] <u>Removing the drill from the machine spindle</u>

48] When the taper shank of the drill is larger than the machine spindle, the device to hold the drill is a...

A] Drill sleeve

B] <u>Taper socket</u>

C] Drill drift

D] Chuck and key

49] A special feature of the radial drilling machine is...

A] It can be used for drilling with a H.S.S] drill
B] Table can be moved and set at any position
C] A variety of speeds is available
D] The spindle can be brought to any position
50] The point angle of drills depends on...
A] The size of the drill
B] The type of machine
C] The material of the work
D] The RPM of the drill
51] The point angle for a standard drill is...
A] 60°
B] 108°
C] 118°
D] 135°
52] The helical angle determines the...
A] Cutting angle
B] Chew angle
C] Rake angle
D] Lip angle
53] The clearance angle of the drill is between...
A] 3° to 5°
B] 8° to 12°
C] 12° to 20°
D] 15° to 20°
54] The relief angle provided behind the cutting edge is called the..
A] Point angle
B] Chisel edge angle
C] Helix angle
D] Clearance angle
55] A set of number drill series consists of drills in the following ranges]
Indicate the correct range
A] 1 to 40
B] 1 to 50
C] 1 to 80
D] 1 to 100
56] In the number drill series, the smallest drill size is...
A] 0.1 mm

B] <u>0.35 mm</u>

C] 0.5 mm

D] 0.52 mm

57] In the number drill series, the largest drill size is...

A] 102 mm

B] <u>5.791 mm</u>

C] 5.613 mm

D] 5.410 mm

58] In the letter drill series, the size of the drill 'A' is equal to ...

A] 13 mm

B] 6.08 mm

C] 6.045 mm

D] <u>5.944 mm</u>

59] In the letter drill series, the largest drill size is equal to...

A] 10.33 mm

B] <u>10.490 mm</u>

C] 12.01 mm

D] 15.00 mm

60] In a remote place (no electricity available] a rail track is to be drilled] Choose the right drilling machine

A] Radial drilling machine

B] Pillar drilling machine

C] <u>Ratchet drilling machine</u>

D] Sensitive drilling Machine

61] A drilling machine used by a carpenter for cabinet making is a...

A] Ratchet drilling machine

B] Radial drilling machine

C] <u>Breast drilling machine</u>

D] Sensitive drilling machine

62] Surface plates are made of...

A] High grade cast steel

B] <u>Fine-grained cast iron</u>

C] Alloy steels

D] Wrought iron

63] The drill size for a M 20 tap is

A] <u>17.5 mm</u>

B] 18 mm

C] 18.5 mm

D] 19 mm

64] Tapping is mostly done to produce

A] external 'V' thread

B] <u>internal 'V' thread</u>

C] external square thread

D] internal square thread

65] The drill size for tapping is

A] more than the tap size

B] <u>less than the tap size</u>

C] equal to the tap size

D] either more or less than the tap size

66] which one of the following is the most suitable tap for lathe work?

A] spiral tap

B] <u>machine tap</u>

C] hand tap

D] left hand tap

67] A die is turned with a

A] die wrench

B] <u>diestock</u>

C] die plate

D] die handle

68] A tumbler gear unit has

A] a single gear

B] two gears

C] <u>three gears</u>

D] four gears

69] The cutting edge of a solid tool is made of

A] <u>carbon steel</u>

B] mild steel

C] super high speed steel

D] stelite

70] The tip of a cemented carbide threading tool is

A] <u>brazed</u>

B] welded

C] soldered

D] clamped to the shank

71] Tool will rub against the work surfaces and the cutting force increases when..

A] The clearance angle is more

B] <u>The clearance angel is less</u>

C] The rake angle is more

D] The rake angle is less

72] Formation of a chip while cutting is based on the...

A] <u>Rake angle of the tool</u>

B] Clearance angle of the tool

C] Wedge angle of the tool

D] Clearance and wedge angle of the tool

73] The suitable cutting fluid for drilling mild steel in a drilling machine is...

A] Synthetic soluble oil

B] Neat oil

C] Distilled water

D] <u>Soluble oil</u>

74] Centre drilling is an operation of...

A] <u>Drilling and countersinking</u>

B] Drilling and counter boring

C] Marking the centre location before drilling

D] Enlarging the diameter of a hole

75] Shaft ends are centre drilled for...

A] <u>Supporting jobs between centres</u>

B] Lubricating the dead centre

C] Reducing the weight

D] Assisting counter boring

76] The Centre drill size is selected on the basis of the

A] length of the job

B] material of the job

C] <u>diameter of the job</u>

D] type of operation

77] Centre drilling is done at a

A] high spindle speed with a high feed

B] low spindle speed with a high feed

C] <u>high spindle speed with a low feed</u>

D] low spindle speed with a low feed

Measuring Instruments in Power System Engineering

78] The least count of vernier caliper is

A] 0.01 mm

B] <u>0.02mm</u>
C] 0.001 mm
D] 0.2 mm

vernier caliper

vernier caliper

Vernier Caliper

79] The graduations of a depth micrometer are...

A] Similar to an outside micrometer

B] <u>In the reverse direction to that of the outside micrometer, both Thimble and sleeve</u>

C] In the reverse direction only on the sleeve

D] In the direction only on the thimble

depth micrometer

depth micrometer

Depth Micrometer

80] The process of enlarging the end of a hole for accommodating the socket screw head is...
A] Reaming
B] Spot facing
C] <u>Counter boring</u>
D] Counter sinking

boring

Boring Operation

81]While choosing a boring tool for boring a given diameter, select

A] a long tool
B] a short tool
C] a long and stout tool
D] a short and stout tool
82] The cutting edge of the boring tool should be set for a small hole so that it is
A] 0.5 mm above the center
B] 0.5 mm below the center
C] 1 mm above the center
D] in the exact center
83] Bored holes are to be chamfered by using
A] a drill
B] triangular scraper
C] a cranked boring tool
D] a flat file
84] The tool used for boring deep holes is a
A] lathe mandrel
B] sleeve
C] drill
D] boring bar
E] auger bit
85] The cutting speed for rough boring is the
A] same as rough turning
B] same as drilling
C] same as knurling
D] same as thread cutting
86] The reamer is used for...
A] Drilling holes in thin sheets
B] Drilling deep holes
C] Removing burrs
D] Enlarging and finishing holes

reamer

reamer

Reamer

87] The reamer teeth are unevenly spaced because...
A] They are easy to manufacture
B] <u>They can reduce chattering</u>
C] They help to cut metal gradually
D] They help to remove the reamer easily
88] Which among the following is not a capability of reamers?
A] Finishing small holes
B] <u>Finishing any machined profiles</u>
C] Accuracy to closer limits
D] Producing high quality surface finish
89] The most important quality of any cutting fluid is
A] emulsification
B] specific heat
C] specific gravity
D] <u>viscosity</u>

cutting fluid 1

Cutting Fluid

90] By using coolants on workpieces we can choose

A] <u>higher cutting speeds</u>

B] lower cutting feeds

C] lower cutting speeds

D] heavy depth of cuts

91] The cutting speed for aluminium with H.S.S] tools is

A] 30 m/min

B] 50 m/min

C] 70 m/min

D] <u>130 m/min</u>

92] The cutting speed for brass with a H.S.S] tool is

A] 10 m/min

B] 25 m/min

C] <u>70 m/min</u>

D] 140 m/min

93] The distance, which the cutting edge of a tool passes over the material in a minute while machining is Know as...

A] RPM

B] Feed

C] Machine speed

D] <u>Cutting speed</u>

94] The cutting angle for chipping cast iron is...

A] 37.5°

B] 55°

C] <u>60°</u>

D] 90°

95] The depth of cut is given by

A] the top slide
B] the cross-slide
C] the compound slide
D] adjusting the tool
96] For mounting a lathe chuck
A] start it by hand and then turn the power on
B] mount it on by power
C] mount it by hand
D] mount it with the help of a hammer
lathe chucks

lathe chuck

Lathe Four Jaw Chuck

97] The morse taper provided on drills used on lathe ranges between
A] MT1 to MT5
B] MT1 to MT4
C] MT0 to MT5
D] MT0 to MT4
98] Feeding the small drill too fast into the work may result in
A] breaking the drill
B] bending the drill

C] cutting an oval shape hole

D] increased production

99] Number of flutes in a twist drills are --------

A] 1

B] 2

C] 3

D] 4

100] Which one of the following drilling machines is used for drilling holes where electricity is not available?

A] Bench drilling machine

B] Pillar drilling machine

C] Redial drilling machine

D] Ratchet drilling machine

101] Which one of the following drilling machine is used for heavy duty work?

A] Bench drilling machine

B] Pillar drilling machine

C] Radial drilling machine

D] Electric hand drilling machine

102] The suitable cutting fluid for drilling mild steel in a lathe is

A] synthetic soluble oil

B] neat cutting oil

C] distilled water

D] soluble oil+water

103] The suitable cutting fluid for precision grinding is

A] Soluble oil

B] Synthetic soluble oil

C] Neat oil

D] Servo Cut's'

gringing wheel   grinding wheel

Grinding Wheel

104] Advantage of using cutting fluid during grinding operation is ------
A] 5000 surface finish
B] Reduction in cutting forces
C] Reduction in hardening of the work piece
D] All of these]
105] Lubricant is necessary to ....]
A] run the machine smoothly taking least load
B] Run the machine quickly
C] Stop the machine immediately
D] Produce work piece of greater accuracy
106] The main purpose for using a lubricant in machine tools is to ------
A] Cool down the making parts
B] Prevent machine tool from heating
C] Wet the making parts for close contact
D] Minimize the friction between the making parts
107] Driving plates are used for
A] mounting fixtures and workpieces
B] driving shafts between Centre's with a lathe dog
C] facing operations only
D] internal operations only
108] Balancing is done in the face plate work
A] to increase the speed
B] to reduce the pressure on the tool
C] for uniform rotation of work
D] to get a good finish
109] A face plate is used to hold
A] a round job
B] a finished job
C] an irregular Job
D] a hollow job
110] Which is correct angle plate used with face plate
(A] Solid Type
(B] Box Type
(C] Adjustable Type
(D] None of them

angle plate

Angle Plate

111] Face plate is made from.....]

(A] Mild Steel

(B] <u>Cast Iron</u>

(C] Brass

(D] Aluminium

112] Which following accessories is use for odd an uneven job turning?

(A] Three Jaw Chuck

(B] Two Jaw Chuck

(C] Driving Plate

(D] <u>Face Plate</u>

113] An irregular shaped work piece is turned on a Lathe] Which one of the following work holding accessories is used?

A] Two Jaw chuck

B] Three Jaw chuck

C] Driving plate

D] <u>Face plate</u>

114]The pads of a steady rest are made of

A] carbon steel

B] lead

C] mild steel

D] <u>brass</u>

steady rest

Steady Rest

115] A steady rest is used
A] to hold jobs
B] for face plate work
C] to drive the job
D] to support the job
116] A follower steady is held on the
A] lathe bed
B] lathe carriage
C] lathe spindle
D] tailstock
117] When turning long work pieces, the following is used
A sleeve
B change gear
C steady rest
D bracket]
118] Knurling operation is done at the
A] turning spindle speed
B] high spindle speed
C] 1/3 of the turning spindle speed
D] 1/2 of the turning spindle speed

knurling tool

Knurling Tool

119] Knurling is the operation of

A] shearing

B] <u>forming</u>

C] turning

D] pressing

120] Mandrels are generally used when machining with

A] heavy cuts

B] <u>short facing cuts</u>

C] light cuts

D] boring tools

Limit Fit & Tolerances in Power System Engineering

121] In the B.I.S system 25 hole deviations are specified by

A] small letters

B] small letters with numbers

C] small letters with tolerance

D] <u>capital letters</u>

122] The standard range of sizes covered in the B.I.S] system of limits and fits are

A] 0 to 10 mm

B] 0 to 100 mm

C] <u>25 to 400 mm</u>

D] 0 to 500 mm

123] The basic size is the size

A] mentioned in the drawing

B] machined by the operator

C] <u>based on which deviations are given</u>

D] given by the instructor

124] Limits of size are

A] <u>2</u>

B] 3

C] 4

D] 5

125] The number of fundamental deviations in the B.I.S] system are

A] 20

B] 22

C] <u>25</u>

D] 28

126] The number of grade of tolerances in the B.I.S] system are

A] 12

B] <u>16</u>

C] 18

D] 20

127] The size based on which the dimensional deviations are given is called...

A] Actual size

B] <u>Basic size</u>

C] Minimum limit of size

D] Maximum limit of Size

128] The size of parts made by .....] for provide interchange ability properties] (A] Measurement System

(B] Trial and Error System

<u>(C] Limit and Tolerance System</u>

(D] None of Them

129] Your job taper is correct if it is measured

A above the higher limit

<u>B in between higher and lower limit</u>

C below the lower limit]

130] When tolerance given in one side of the basic dimension, it is called ---------

A].Tolerance system

<u>B] Unilateral tolerance</u>

C] Bilateral tolerance

D] Allowance System

131] A dimension is stated as (025 H7 in a drawing] The lower limit is -----------

A] 24.75 mm

B] 24.85 mm

C] 25.00 mm

D] 25-021 mm

132] The measured Size Of the dimensions of a component as called---------

A] Basic size

B] Nominal Size

C] Allowed size

D] Actual size

133] In the drawing the dimensions of a shaft is shown 40i 0068/0042, which is the size of Shaft within the tolerance?

A] 4.0.64 mm

B] 40.042 mm

C] 40.000 mm

D] 39.998 mm

134] In Hole basic system ----------

A] The size of the shaft is made constant

B] The Size of the hole is made constant

C] Only 'allowance is given on the hole

D] The permissible tolerance are given on the hole and the Shaft

135] The Size of a component is given as 24 -0.1] What does -O.1 indicates? _

A] Upper deviation is + 0.1 mm]

B] Lower deviation is 0.0 mm

C] Fundamental deviation is 0.0 mm

D] Lower deviation is _0.1 mm

136] The tolerance of a hole iS the difference between the -------

A] Maximum hole Size and maximum Shaft size

B] Maximum hole size and maximum hole Size

C] Minimum'hole size and maximum Shaft Size

D] Minimum hole Size and minimum shaft Size

137] A hole whose lower deviation is zero is called basic hole] Which one of the following letter indicates basic hole?]

A] E

B] F

C] G '

D] H

138] Which one having upper deviation zero?

A] Bassc Shaft

B] Basic hole

C] Tolerance

D] Clearance

139] A ball bearing on a shaft is type of fit? ,

A] Clearance fit

B] Driving fit

C] Shrinkage fit

D] None of the above

140] Which one of the following is important factor required to achieve the interchange ability in mass production?]

A] Geometrical accuracy]

B] Standardization

C] Dimensional accuracy

D] Surface finish

141] In the BIS system of limits and fits, the grade of tolerance are represented by number Symbols and there are ---------i

A] 14 grades of tolerance

B] 16 grades of tolerance

C] 18 grades of tolerance '

D] 20 grades of tolerance

142] A Product is said to have the quality when ....]

A] Its shape and dimensions are within the limit

B] It is fit for use

C] It appears to be very good

D] The choice of material is right

143] The maximum clearance required between hole'30 +0.021, 0.000 and shaft 30 -0.110, 0.143 is.

A] 0.110 mm '

B]0.131 mm

C] 0.164 mm

D] 0.143 mm

144] A dimension is stated as 25 .1002 mm in a drawing] What is the tolerance?

A] +0.02 mm'

B] +0.04 mm

C] -0.02 mm

D] 25.00 mm

145] A pin is fitted in a hole] The tolerance zone of the pin is entirely above that of hole] The fit obtained will be?

A] Clearance fit

B] Transition fit

<u>C] Interference fit</u>

D] Running fit

146] Interchange ability is normally applied for? _

A] Repairing of parts

<u>B] Mass production</u>

C] Single piece production

D] All of these

147] Tolerance is given to the part size to............]

<u>A] Production the part within the required permissible size error</u>

B] Increase the production

C] Decrease the Production

D] Finish the components approximately

148] Which one of the following is the clearance fit under the whole basic system?

A] 20 H7/p6'

B] 2067/211

C] ZOG/gll]

<u>D] 20H/g11]</u>

149] The three classes of fits as per BIS system aré ....] ~]

<u>A] Clearance fit, interference fit and transition fit</u>

B] Medium fit, push fit and tight fit

C] Flat fit, round fit and square fit

D] 'Sliding fit ', loose fit and shrinkage fit

150] Which one of the following tolerance specifications has a maximum dimensionless than 20 mm?

A] 20 +0.2,-0.3

B] 20 320.2

<u>C] 20 -0.2, 0.3 e</u>

D]m 20 +500, ~03

151] Difference between the maximum and minimum limit is -~-~~~~-~~~~~ '

A] Single informant

B] Basic shaft

C] Clearance

D] Tolerance

152] A shaft 55 running freely in bush bearing the type of fit is ---------

A] Clearance fit

B] Driving plate

C] shrinkage fit

D] None of the above

153] The taper ratio of the morse taper is

A] 1 in 10

B] 1 in 15

C] 1 in 20

D] 1 in 25

154] The morse standard taper is available in

A] 16 Nos

B] 12 Nos

C] 10 Nos

D] 8 Nos

155] Taper turning by offsetting the tailstock method can produce

A] an internal taper

B] an internal taper thread

C] an external taper

D] both external and internal tapers

taper turning

taper turning attachment

Taper by Tailstock Offset

156] By using the taper turning attachment, tapers can be turned with a setting angle up to

A] 10°

B] 15°

C] 20°

D] 30°

157] The accuracy of a taper is generally checked by means of......

A] taper gauges

B] gauge blocks

C] indicator and height gauge

D] 'V' blocks

158] Turning tapers by the compound rest method involves working solely with

Decimal measurements

B fractional measurements

C metric measurements

D angular measurements]

159] Long tapers are produced

A with the taper turning attachment

B with the compound slide

C by setting over the tail stock

D by adjusting the cross slide]

160] The length of turned tapers are checked with

A vernier calliper

B micrometer

C inside callper

D dial test indicator]

161] The disadvantages of taper turning using the com] pound slide are

A] only long tapers can be turned

B] only very large tapers can be turned

C] only manual in feed is possible

D] only short tapers can be turned due to the restrictions of the compound slide]

162] External tapers are checked with

A] limit plug gauge

B] taper ring gauge

C]taper plug gauge

D] thread plug gauge]

163] The use of a taper turned on lathe is ----

A] Assist to transmit drive in the assembled parts

B] Used for Assembly and disassembly of parts

C] Give self alignment in the assembled parts

164] Which type of method is used in mass production of production of producing small length of taper?

A] Form tool

B] Compound slide

C] Tailstock offset.

D] Taper turning attachment

165] Morse standard taper is one of the internationally accepted standards taper, which is available in numbers from--------

A]1to7

B]1 to 8

C] O to 7

D] 0 to 8

166] Which taper turning method is used for cutting steep taper?

A] Set over method

B] Taper turning attachment

C] Form tool

D] Swivelling the compound rest

167] Morse taper is used in which of the following machine components -...

A] Spindles of lathe

B] Spindles of drill machine

C] Shanks of reamers

D] All of these

168] For mass production of the taper which one of the following method is used.......]

A] Tailstock offset method

B] Taper turning attachment method

C] Form too method

D] Compound slide method

169] The major diameter of the taper is 40 mm, minor diameter is 30 mm] The total length of the job is 100 mm is tapered then offset is given by -

A] 5 mm

B] 7.5 mm

C] 12 mm

D] 9 mm

170] The accuracy of an ordinary bevel protractor is --' -----------degree]

A] One

B] Three

C] Two

D] Four

171] The least count of a vernier bevel protractor is...

A] 1"

B] <u>5'</u>

C] 1°

D] 5 °

172] The part of a vernier bevel protractor which is normally used as a reference base for measuring angles is the...

A] Blade

B] <u>Stock</u>

C] Disc

C] Main scale

173] The part of a vernier bevel protector on which main scale divisions are marked is the...

A] Stock

B] Dial

C] <u>Disc</u>

D] Adjustable blade

174] The part of a bevel protractor, which comes in contact with the inclined surface while measuring is the...

A] <u>Blade</u>

B] Stock

C] Disc

D] Dial

175] The value of each division of the main scale of a vernier bevel protractor is...

A] 5'

B] <u>1°</u>

C] 5°

D.10°

176] The value of each division of the vernier scale of a bevel protractor is...

A] 1°

B] 1°5'

C] <u>1°55'</u>

D.5'

177] The part of the vernier bevel protractor on which main scale divisions are marked

A stock

<u>B dial</u>

C disc

D adjustable blade

178] In Vernier bevel protractor is designed to measure?

A] Acute angles

B] Obtuse angles

<u>C] Acute and Obtuse angle</u>

D] Liner dimensions

179] To get least count of 5 in a vernier bevel protractor the 23° main scale are divided into -..

<u>A] 12 equal parts on vernier scale</u>

B] 22 equal parts on vernier scale

C] 24 equal parts on vernier scale

D] 25 equal parts on vernier scale

180] Which of the following is not the part of a combination set?

<u>A] Stock</u>

B] Square head

C] Protractor head

D] Centre head

181] The datum, form which the measurements of the vernier height gauge are taken, is...

A] The beam

B] The vernier slide

C] <u>The base</u>

D] Above the scriber poing

vernier height gauge   vernier height guage

Vernier Height Gauge

182]The part of a vernier height gauge on which the main scale divisions are graduated is the...

A] Base

B] <u>Beam</u>

C] Fine setting device

D] The vernier plate

183] On which part of the vernier height gauge are the main scale division graduated?]

A] Base

B] Vernier plate

C] <u>Beam</u>

D] Fine adjusting unit

184] For marking purpose a Vernier height gauge must be on the --------

A] Bed of a machine tool

B] <u>Surface plate</u>

C] Square block

D] Any flat surface

185] Before using Vernier height gauge make sure that the --------

A] Locking screw is in a locked position

B] Scriber is Locked

C] <u>Zero of the vernier coincides with zero of the main scale</u>

D] Gib is Provided

186] The least count Of a vernier height gauge is...........]

A] 0.05 mm

B] 0.1 mm

C] <u>0.02 mm</u>

D] 0001 mm

187] Which laying out the vernier height gauge must be used on the ----------

A] V block

B] Machine bed

C] Surface plate

D] Any flat surface

188] The part which is slides on the beam of a vernier height gauge is known as a ------

A] Base

B] Beam scale

C] Scriber

D] Vernier slide

189] The base of the vernier height gauge is generally made out of ----------

A] Cast iron]

B] Steel

C] Aluminium alloy

D] Tungsten carbide

190] Which instrument iis used for marking layout?

A] Micrometer

B] Vernier

C] Depth gauge

D] Vernier height gauge

191] While marking with a Vernier height gauge, the work piece is generally ----------

A] Supported by an angle plate

B] Supported by another work piece

C] Held by one hand

D] Held without support

192] Which of the following is not the part of a combination set?

A] Stock

B] Square head

C] Protractor head

D] Centre head

Electrical MCQ for Power System Engineering

85] A heater draws a current of 8A when connected to a 240V source] What is the resistance value of the heater element in ohms?

A] 40

B] 20

C] <u>30</u>

D] 60

86] An electric soldering iron with an 80 ohms heating element is plugged into a 240V outlet] How much current will be drawn by the iron?

A] 2A

B] <u>3A</u>

C] 4A

D] 5A

87] The alternator in a car delivers 4A and has a load of 3 ohms connected across its terminals] Find the voltage of the circuit

A] 18V

B] 24V

C] <u>12V</u>

D] 16V

88] Three resistors of 1K ohms, 2K ohms and 7K ohms are connected in series with a 30 V supply] If 2 K ohms and 7 K ohms resistors are open circuited, a voltmeter connected across the 7K ohms resistor will indicate...

A] 10 k ohms, 3A

B] 10 k ohms, 300mA

C] <u>10 k ohms, 3 mA</u>

D] 5 k ohms, 6 mA

89] A voltage source produces an IR drop of 40V across a 20 ohms resistance, 60V across a 30 ohms resistance and 180V across a 90 ohms resistance all in series] How much is the applied voltage?

A] 180 V

B] 240 V

C] 100 V

D] <u>280 V</u>

90] Three resistors 27 ohms, 47 ohms and 68 ohms are connected in parallel] What is the otal resistance?

A] <u>less than 27 ohms</u>

B] greater than 68 ohms

C] between 27 and 47 ohms

D] sum of all the three resistances

91] One million and one mege ohms resistors are there if connected both in parallel, what would be the combined resistance value?

A] <u>0.5 mega ohm</u>

B] 0.5 milli ohm

C] 0.5 kilo ohm

D] 0.5 ohm

92] A 24 ohms and a 8 ohms resistors in parallel gets a combined resistance of...

A] <u>6 ohms</u>

B] 12 ohms

C] 3 ohms

D] 32 ohms

93] Resistors of the following values are connected in parallel, 5 ohms, 5 kilo-ohms, 50 kilo-ohms, 5 mega ohms] Their equivalent resistance will be very near to...

A] <u>4.5 ohms</u>

B] 4500 ohms

C] 45000 ohms

D] 4,500,000 ohms

94] The resistance of given wire is 2 ohms] The resistance of the other wire made of the same material having twice the length and twice the cross sectional area is...

A] 5 ohms

B] 6 ohms

C] <u>2 ohms</u>

D] 8 ohms

95] If the area of a metal wire of a given length is doubles, its resistance will...

A] be doubled

B] <u>be halved</u>

C] remain the same

D] be four times more

96].Among the following only one is regarded as resistance wire

A] gold

B] silver

C] <u>nichrome</u>

D] copper

97] Arc heating occurs when the air between electrodes of opposite polarity becomes..

A] moistened

B] dry

C] <u>ionized</u>
D] none of the above
98] The meter used to measure the temperature of furnace is...
A] hydrometer
B] <u>pyrometer</u>
C] hygrometer
D] tachometer
99] in the case of electrolyte a rise in temperature causes...
A] <u>decrease in resistance</u>
B] increase in resistance
C] no change in resistance
D] none of the above
100] Heat developed in a conductor is proportional to the...
A] square of the power
B] square of the resistance
C] <u>square of the current</u>
D] square of the time
101] Out of the four metal/alloys given below, one has almost no change in resistance for temperature change...
A] nickel
B] nichrome
C] platinum
D] <u>manganin</u>
102] A material that is slightly repelled by a magnet is called ...
A] magnetic
B] paramagnetic
C] <u>diamagnetic</u>
D] ferromagnetic
103] A material that can be magnetized only very slightly is called...
A] magnetic
B] <u>paramagnetic</u>
C] diamagnetic
D] ferromagnetic
104] Substances that can be magnetized easily and make very strong magnets are called...
A] <u>ferromagnetic</u>
B] diamagnetic
C] paramagnetic

D] permanent magnetic

105] A substance that has a high retentivity can be used for the manufacture of...

A] electromagnets

B] <u>permanent magnets</u>

C] temporary magnets

D] paramagnets

106] A substance that has low retentivity can be used for the manufacture of...

A] <u>electromagnets</u>

B] permanent magnets

C] bar magnets

D] paramagnets

107] The symbol for inductance is...

A] H

B] I

C] <u>L</u>

D] X

108] Tube lamp choke is the best example of...

A] open circuited

B] <u>short circuited</u>

C] grounded

D] connected to the neutral line

109] The initial function of a choke in a tube light circuit is to...

A] limit the starting current

B] <u>induce high voltage</u>

C] heat up the filament

D] limit the current after starting

110] The second function of a choke in a tube light circuit is to...

A] limit the starting current

B] induce high voltage

C] heat up the filament

D] <u>limit the current after starting</u>

111] The periodic time of a wave from is 2ms] Calculate the frequency

A] 50 HZ

B] 5 HZ

C] <u>500HZ</u>

D] 5 KHZ

112] How big is the peak amplitude of a sine-wave with an effective value of 220 volts?

A] <u>311 V</u>

B] 380 V

C] 400 V

D] 440 V

113] The peak-to-peak voltage is 99V] how big is the effective value of the sine wave?

A] 70 V

B] 44.5V

C] 49.5 V

D] <u>35 V</u>

114] A moving coil voltmeter reads 10 V AC] How big is the effective voltage?

A] higher

B] lower

C] <u>the same</u>

D] 10% higher

115] A moving iron ammeter reads 10 A] how big is the peak current of the oscillation?

A] 7.07 A

B] 1.1414A

C] 70.7 A

D] <u>14.1 A</u>

116] A current of 2 amps flows through a resistance of 10 ohms] The power dissipated in the resistance is equal to...

A] 20 watts

B] 200 watts

C] <u>40 watts</u>

D] 5 watts

117] If the frequency changes from 50 HZ to 100 HZ keeping voltage constant, the inductive reactance of coil connected to supply...

A] remains same

B] become half

C] <u>become doubled</u>

D] become 4 times

118] Capacitance is not affected by...

A] plate area

B] distance between plates

C] dialectic material

D] <u>frequency</u>

119] The capacitive reactance of a capacitor varies...

A] directly with frequency

B] <u>inversely with frequency</u>

C] directly with applied voltage

D] inversely with applied voltage

120] A capacitor acquired 3 coulombs of charge when 6 volts are applied across it] It has a capacitance of ...

A] <u>0.5 farad</u>

B] 3 farads

C] 3 farads

D] 18 farads

121] A capacitor is connected across a 200 volt AC line, its minimum voltage rating should be...

A] 100 volts

B] 200 Volts

C] <u>300 volts</u>

D] 400 volts

122] when testing a capacitor with an ohmmeter, the meter indicates some resistance] The capacitor under test is...

A] <u>leaky</u>

B] open

C] good

D] short

123] The total capacitance of a 40 micro farad capacitor connected in series with an 80 micro farad capacitor is...

A] <u>26.7 micro farad</u>

B] 40 micro farad

C] 60.6 micro farad

D] 120 micro farad

124] For obtaining 1 micro farad capacitor from 3 nos] of 3 micro farad capacitors we have to connect...

A] all in parallel

B] <u>all in series</u>

C] 2 series and one in parallel

D] none of the above

125] In an AC series circuit having R and C the current flowing through the capacitor will be...
A] lagging the voltage
B] <u>leading the voltage</u>
C] in phase with the voltage
D] none of the above

126] If the frequency of the supply is increased in the R-C series circuit the capacitive reactance will be
A] <u>reduced</u>
B] increased
C] having no effect
D] none of the above

127] Power companies are interested in improving the power factor to
A] <u>reduce line current</u>
B] increase motor efficiency
C] increase volt-amperes
D] decrease power

128] A capacitor increases the power factor value of an AC motor load when it is connected...
A] in series with the motor
B] in series with the starter
C] <u>in parallel with the motor</u>
D] in series with the main winding

129] Normally, the power factor of an incandescent lighting circuit is..
A] 0
B] 0.5
C] 0.707
D] <u>1.0</u>

130] When resistance alone is used to determine current in an RLC series circuit, the circuit is...
A] an inductive circuit
B] a capacitive circuit
C] a combination circuit
D] <u>a resonant circuit</u>

131] Inductive reactance is directly related to..
A] resistance
B] <u>frequency</u>
C] capacitance

D] power

132] Synchronous motor when used for power factor improvement should be...

A] under excited

B] <u>over excited</u>

C] loaded

D] running at no load

133] In a RL parallel circuit, the opposition to total current is called...

A] reactance

B] resistance

C] a vector sum

D] <u>impedance</u>

134] In a AC parallel RL circuit, the power dissipated at the

A] impedance

B] <u>resistance</u>

C] inductance

D] capacitance

135] How much is the nominal output voltage of a carbon zinc cell?

A] 12V

B] <u>1.5V</u>

C] 2.0V

D] 2.2V

136] Cells are connected in series to..

A] <u>increase the output voltage</u>

B] decreases the output voltage

C] decrease the internal resistance

D] increase the current capacity

54137connected in

A] series

B] <u>parallel</u>

C] series-parallel

D] parallel-series

138] The capacity of a cell is measured in

A] watt-hour

B] watts

C] amperes

D] <u>ampere-hour</u>

139] The primary cell which has the shortest shelf life is

A] <u>carbon – zinc</u>

B] alkaline

C] mercury

D] lithium

140] The cell which has very high energy density for given weight or volume to

A] carbon-zinc

B] alkaline

C] mercury

D] <u>lithium</u>

141] A 100-Ah capacity battery should deliver a current of 8A for approximately...

A] <u>12 h</u>

B] 8 h

C] 20 h

D] 100 h

142] When the battery is needed to be kept idle for a long time...

A] overcharge the battery

B] remove electrolyte

C] clean the plates with distilled water

D] <u>dry them and store the battery in cool dry clean place</u>

143] The active materials of the nickel iron cell are...

A] nickel hydroxide

B] powdered iron and its oxide

C] 21% solution of caustic potash

D] <u>all the above materials</u>

144] The capacity of a cell is measured in

A] watt hour

B] watts

C] amperes

D] <u>ampere-hour</u>

145] To charge a secondary cell, the system used is

A] low voltage AC

B] high voltage AC

C] AC

D] <u>DC</u>

146] What is the number of phases in a normal industrial supply system?

A] one

B] <u>three</u>

C] four

D] two

147] In a 3 phase star connected alternator, the coils have a phase difference of...

A] <u>120°</u>

B] 240°

C] 60°

D] 360°

148] Delta connection is used no one of the following

A] primary of the transmission line transformer

B] alternator winding

C] secondary of the distribution transformer

D] <u>primary of the distribution transformer</u>

149] Which method can be used to measure the power in a 3-phase unbalanced load system?

A] one wattmeter method

B]<u> tow wattmeter method</u>

C] three wattmeter method

D] three ammeter method

150] Two wattmeters can be used to measure 3-hase power in a 3-phase, 3 wire system with...

A] balanced load

B] unbalanced load

C] <u>balanced as well as unbalanced load</u>

D] out of balanced load

151] A single wattmeter can be used to measure power in a 3-phase system only when the load is..

A] <u>balanaced</u>

B] unbalanced

C] balanced as well as unbalanced load

D] constant

152] The force producing movement of the pointer in an indicating instrument is called as...

A] <u>deflecting force</u>

B] controlling force

C] damping force

D] distracting force

153] A permanent magnet moving coil instrument will read...
A] only AC quantities
B] only DC quantities
C] both AC and DC quantities
D] pulsating quantities

154] An instrument using gravity control will read correctly if used in..
A] vertical position only
B] horizontal position only
C] inclined position only
D] any position

155] Which one of the following damping methods is used in permanent magnet moving coil instrument?
A] air damping
B] fluid damping
C] spring damping
D] eddy current damping

156] Moving coil instrument works on the effect of...
A] chemical effect
B] heating effect
C] electrostatic effect
D] electromagnetic effect

157] The meter installed at your house to measure electrical energy is an example of...
A] indication type instrument
B] recording type instrument
C] indicating as well as recording type instrument
D] integrating type instrument

158].Which of the following material is preferred for permanent magnet?
A] alnico
B] y-alloy
C] silicon steel
D] wrought iron

159] The instrument which could be classified as absolute instrument is...
A] milli ammeter
B] micro ammeter
C] galvanometer

D] <u>tangent galvanomer</u>

160] Which of the following methods of damping is commonly used in moving iron instrument?

A] <u>Air damping</u>

B] fluid damping

C] eddy current damping

D] viscosity damping

161] The deflecting torque of a moving iron instrument is directly proportional to the..

A] current

B] <u>square of the current</u>

C] square root of the current

D] voltage

162]Which of the following is used for measuring the medium resistance directly?

A] ammeter

B] <u>megger</u>

C] ohmmeter

D] voltmeter

163] An ohmmeter is used for measuring the...

A] insulation resistance

B] <u>resistance</u>

C] current

D] potential difference

164] Which of the following components is not a part of an ohmmeter?

A] fixed resistor

B] variable resistor

C] <u>capacitor</u>

D] battery

165] In shunt ohmmeter, maximum deflection signifies ..

A] <u>maximum resistance</u>

B] minimum resistance

C] a fault in the megger

D] none of these

166].An unknown DC voltage is to be measured, which measuring range will you select first?

A] <u>500V</u>

B] 50V

C] 1.5 V

D] 0.5V

167].An unknown direct current of micro ampere rating is to be measured, which measuring range will you select first?

A] 20 micro amp

B] 15 micro amp

C] 150 micro amp

D] 500 micro amp

168] A multimeter cannot measure...

A] current

B] potential difference

C] capacitance

D] resistance

169] Dynamometer type meters are used to measure...

A] only AC quantities

B] only DC quantities

C] both AC and DC

D] pulsating AC only

170] Which effect is used in wattmeter?

A] electrodynamic effect

B] thermal effect

C] chemical effect

D] electrostatic effect

171] Which of the instrument listed below operates efficiently as wattmeter in both AC and DC?

A] PMMC instrument

B] dynamometer instrument

C] hot wire instrument

D] MI instrument

172] Electrodynamic type of instrument are used commonly for the measurement of...

A] voltage

B] current

C] resistance D]

173] When the phase and neutral of the energy meter are interchanged, its disc...

A] rotates in reverse direction

B] rotates in correct direction

C] will stop

D] rotates slowly

E] rotates at high speed

174] When the disc of energy meter is rotating even without connecting any load, the error is called

A] creeping error

B] phase error

C] friction error

D] temperature error

175] AC single phase energy meters record the energy in the unit of...

A] kilowatt hours

B] number of thousands of disc rotation

C] volt amperes

D] kilo volt ampere

176] A megger measures resistance in...

A] ohms

B] hundreds of ohms

C] thousands of ohms

D] millions of ohms

177] A megger is exclusively designed for measuring..

A] very high resistance

B] very low resistance

C] ground faults in power lines

D] over loads on DC motors

178] For pipe earthing the minimum internal diameter of galvanized iron of steel pipe required is...

A] 12.5 mm

B] 16mm

C] 3.5 mm

D] 4 m

179] The earth conductor provides a path to ground for..

A] leakage current

B] over current

C] high voltage

D] circuit current

180] if the size of the circuit copper conductor is 10 sq-mm then the size of earth conductor in G.I] wire should be...

A] 1.5 sq.mm

B] 2.5 sq.mm

C] 5 sq.mm

D] 10 sq.mm

181] One calory is equal to,,,

A] 4187 joules

B] 418.7 joules

C] 41.87 joules

D] 4.187 joules

182] The operating temperature range of electrical stove with bare heating element is...

A] 300° to 400°C

B] 500° to 600°C

C] 550° to 900°C

D] 1100° to 1300°C

183] Which appliance works on heating effect of electric current?

A] incandescent lamp

B] bimetallic thermostat

C] H R C fuse

D] toaster

184] What is the size of nichrome wire for heating element of 1000 watts, 230V heater at 500°C?

A] 18 SWG

B] 20SWG

C] 24 SWG

D] 25 SWG

185] The heat proof insulating material used for heater base is...

A] mica

B] porcelain

C] asbestos

D] glass wool

186].The temperature regulating component of an automatic electric iron is...

A] heating element

B] thermostat

C] sole plate

D] pressure plate

187].The bread toasting zone temperature is about...

A] 400∘C

B] 800∘C

C] 260∘C

D] 975∘C

188] If a winding makes electrical contact with the metal case of the mixer motor the winding is...

A] grounded

B] open circuited

C] short circuited

D] loose connected

189] If the end shafts of a rotor turns blue it is an indication of...

A] scoring

B] overheating

C] freezing

D] burring

190] What type of motor is used in a food mixer?

A] DC shunt motor

B] universal motor

C] capacitor start motor

D] capacitor start and run motor

191] In what position is the motor mounted in most of the mixers?

A] vertical

B] horizontal

C] inclined

D] parallel

Fluid Mechanics MCQ for Power System Engineering

1. Which one is in a state of failure?

a) Solid

b) Liquid

c) Gas

d) Fluid

2. A small shear force is applied on an element and then removed. If the element regains it's original position, what kind of an element can it be?

a) Solid

b) Liquid

c) Fluid

d) Gaseous

3. In which type of matter, one won't find a free surface?

a) Solid
b) Liquid
c) <u>Gas</u>
d) Fluid

4. If a person studies about a fluid which is at rest, what will you call his domain of study?
a) Fluid Mechanics
b) <u>Fluid Statics</u>
c) Fluid Kinematics
d) Fluid Dynamics

5. The value of the compressibility of an ideal fluid is
a) <u>zero</u>
b) unity
c) infinity
d) more than that of a real fluid

6. The value of the Bulk Modulus of an ideal fluid is
a) zero
b) unity
c) <u>infinity</u>
d) less than that of a real fluid

7. The value of the viscosity of an ideal fluid is
a) <u>zero</u>
b) unity
c) infinity
d) more than that of a real fluid

8. The value of the surface tension of an ideal fluid is
a) <u>zero</u>
b) unity
c) infinity
d) more than that of a real fluid

9. Which of the following statement is true about vapor pressure of a liquid?
a) <u>Vapor pressure is closely related to molecular activity and temperature of the liquid</u>
b) Vapor pressure is closely related to molecular activity but independent of the temperature of the liquid
c) Vapor pressure is not affected by molecular activity and temperature of the liquid

d) Vapor pressure is not affected by molecular activity and is independent of the temperature of the liquid

10. Which of the following equation correctly depicts the relation between the vapor pressure of a liquid and it's temperature?

a) Vapor pressure increases linearly with the increase in temperature of the liquid

b) <u>Vapor pressure increases slightly with the increase in temperature of the liquid at low temperatures and the rate of increase goes high at higher temperatures</u>

c) Vapor pressure increases rapidly with the increase in temperature of the liquid at low temperatures and the rate of increase goes low at higher temperatures

d) Vapor pressure remains unchanged with the increase in temperature of the liquid

11. Which of the following is the condition for the boiling of a liquid?

a) Absolute pressure of a liquid must be greater than or equal to it's vapor pressure

b) <u>Absolute pressure of a liquid must be less than or equal to it's vapor pressure</u>

c) Absolute pressure of a liquid must be equal to it's vapor pressure

d) Absolute pressure of a liquid must be greater than it's vapor pressure

12. Which of the following machines have the possibility of cavitation?

a) <u>Reaction turbines and centrifugal pumps</u>

b) Reaction turbines and reciprocating pumps

c) Impulse turbines and centrifugal pumps

d) Impulse turbines and reciprocating pumps

13. The three liquids 1, 2, and 3 with vapor pressures V1, V2 and V3 respectively, are kept under same pressure. If V1 > V2 > V3, which liquid will start boiling early?

a) <u>liquid 1</u>

b) liquid 2

c) liquid 3

d) they will start boiling at the same time

14. Equal amount of a particular liquid is poured into three similar containers, namely 1, 2 and 3, at a temperature of T1, T2 and T3 respectively. If T1 < T2 < T3, the liquid in which container will have the highest vapor pressure?

a) container 1

b) container 2

c) <u>container 3</u>

d) the vapor pressure of the liquid will remain the same irrespective of it's temperature

15. The absolute pressure of a water is 0.5kN above it's vapor pressure. If it flows with a velocity of 1m/s, what will be the value of Cavitation Number describing the flow induced boiling?

a) 0.25

b) 0.5

c) <u>1</u>

d) 2

16. Which of the following is correct regarding the formation and collapse of vapor bubbles in a liquid?

a) Vapor bubbles are formed when the fluid pressure goes above the vapor pressure and collapses when the fluid pressure goes above the bubble pressure

b) Vapor bubbles are formed when the fluid pressure goes above the vapor pressure and collapses when the fluid pressure goes below the bubble pressure

c) Vapor bubbles are formed when the fluid pressure drops below the vapor pressure and collapses when the fluid pressure goes below the bubble pressure

d) <u>Vapor bubbles are formed when the fluid pressure drops below the vapor pressure and collapses when the fluid pressure goes above the bubble pressure</u>

Thermodynamics MCQ for Power System Engineering

1. A piston/cylinder with a cross-sectional area of 0.01 m^2 is resting on the stops. With an outside pressure of 100 kPa, what should be the water pressure to lift the piston?

a) 178kPa

b) 188kPa

c) <u>198kPa</u>

d) 208kPa

3. A large exhaust fan in a lab room keeps the pressure inside at 10 cm water relative vacuum to the hallway? What is the net force acting on the door measuring 1.9 m by 1.1 m?

a) 2020 N

b) 2030 N

c) 2040 N

d) <u>2050 N</u>

4. A 5 m long vertical tube having cross sectional area 200 cm^2 is placed in a water. It is filled with 15°C water, with the bottom closed and the top open to 100 kPa atmosphere. How much water is present in tube?

a) <u>99.9 kg</u>

b) 109.9 kg

c) 89.9 kg

d) 79.9 kg

5. A 5 m long vertical tube having cross sectional area 200 cm2 is placed in a water. It is filled with 15°C water, with the bottom closed and the top open to 100 kPa atmosphere. What is the pressure at the bottom of tube ?

a) 119 kPa

b) 129 kPa

c) 139 kPa

d) <u>149 kPa</u>

6. Find the pressure of water at 200°C and having specific volume of 1.5 m3/kg.

a) <u>0.9578 m3/kg</u>

b) 0.8578 m3/kg

c) 0.7578 m3/kg

d) 0.6578 m3/kg

7. Find the pressure of water at 200°C and having specific volume of 1.5 m^3/kg.

a) 141.6 kPa

b) 111.6 kPa

c) 121.6 kPa

d) <u>161.6 kPa</u>

8. A 5m^3 container is filled with 840 kg of granite (density is 2400 kg/m^3) and the rest of the volume is air (density is 1.15 kg/m^3). Find the mass of air present in the container.

a) 9.3475 kg

b) 8.3475 kg

c) 6.3475 kg

d) <u>5.3475 kg</u>

9. A 100 m tall building receives superheated steam at 200 kPa at ground and leaves saturated vapour from the top at 125 kPa by losing 110 kJ/kg of heat. What should be the minimum inlet temperature at the ground of the

building so that no steam will condense inside the pipe at steady state?

a) 363.54°C

b) 263.54°C

c) <u>163.54°C</u>

d) none of the mentioned

10. The pressure gauge on an air tank shows 60 kPa when the diver is 8 m down in the ocean. At what depth will the gauge pressure be zero?

a) 34.118 m

b) <u>24.118 m</u>

c) 14.118 m

d) none of the mentioned

11. A piston-cylinder device initially contains air at 150 kPa and 27°C. At this state, the volume is 400 litre. The mass of the piston is such that a 350 kPa pressure is required to move it. The air is now heated until its volume has doubled. Determine the final temperature.

a) <u>1400 K</u>

b) 400 K

c) 500 K

d) 1500 K

12. A piston-cylinder device initially contains air at 150 kPa and 27°C. At this state, the volume is 400 litre. The mass of the piston is such that a 350 kPa pressure is required to move it. The air is now heated until its volume has doubled. Determine work done by the air.

a) 120 kJ

b) 130 kJ

c) 100 kJ

d) <u>140 kJ</u>

13. Find the change in u for carbon dioxide between 600 K and 1200 K for a constant Cv0 value.

a) 291.8 kJ/kg

b) <u>391.8 kJ/kg</u>

c) 491.8 kJ/kg

d) 591.8 kJ/kg

14. Calculate the change in enthalpy of carbon dioxide from 30 to 1500°C at 100 kPa at constant specific heat.

a) 2237.7 kJ/kg

b) 1637.7 kJ/kg

c) <u>1237.7 kJ/kg</u>

d) 2337.7 kJ/kg

15. A sealed rigid vessel has volume of 1 m3 and contains 2 kg of water at 100°C. The vessel is now heated. If a safety pressure valve is installed, at what pressure should the valve be set to have a maximum temperature of 200°C ?

    a) <u>431.3 kPa</u>

    b) 531.3 kPa

    c) 631.3 kPa

    d) 731.3 kPa

16. A system undergoing change in state from A to B along path 'X' receives 100 J heat and does 40 J work. It returns to state A from B along path 'Y' with work input of 30 J. Calculate the heat transfer involved along the path 'Y'.

    a) – 60 J

    b) 60 J

    c) <u>– 90 J</u>

    d) 90 J

17. Which of the following were used as fixed points before 1954?

    a) The ice point

    b) The steam point

    c) <u>All of the mentioned</u>

    d) None of the mentioned

18. What is the standard fixed point of thermometry?

    a) The ice point

    b) The steam point

    c) <u>The triple point of water</u>

    d) None of the mentioned

19. All gases and vapours approach ideal gas behaviour at?

    a) High pressure and high density

    b) <u>Low pressure and low density</u>

    c) High pressure and low density

    d) Low pressure and high density

20. The value of ratio of the steam point temperature to the ice point temperature is?

    a) 1.466

    b) 1.266

    c) 1.166

    d) <u>1.366</u>

21. Celsius temperature of the triple point of water is (in degree Celsius)?

a) -0.00

b) 0.00

c) <u>0.01</u>

d) None of the mentioned

22. Which of the following is chosen as the standard thermometric substance?

a) <u>Gas</u>

b) Liquid

c) Solid

d) All of the mentioned

23. A real gas behaves as an ideal gas when?

a) Temperature approaches zero

b) <u>Pressure approaches zero</u>

c) Both temperature and pressure approaches zero

d) None of the mentioned

24. The temperature interval from the oxygen point to the gold point is divided into how many parts?

a) 2

b) <u>3</u>

c) 4

d) 1

Microprocessor MCQ for Power System Engineering

1. The interconnection topologies are implemented using __________ as a node.

a) control unit

b) microprocessor

c) processing unit

d) <u>microprocessor or processing unit</u>

2. The feature of the multi-microprocessor architecture is

a) task dependent

b) single bus provider for many processors

c) design is for a specific task

d) <u>all of the mentioned</u>

3. The main objective in building the multi-microprocessor is

a) greater throughput

b) enhanced fault tolerance

c) <u>greater throughput and enhanced fault tolerance</u>

d) none of the mentioned

4. An interface between the user or an application program, and the system resources are

a) microprocessor

b) microcontroller

c) multi-microprocessor

d) <u>operating system</u>

5. An operating system provides

a) hardware and software resource management

b) input/output management

c) memory management

d) <u>all of the mentioned</u>

6. Distributed systems are designed to run

a) serial process

b) parallel process

c) serial and parallel process

d) <u>none of the mentioned</u>

7. A distributed operating system must provide a mechanism for

a) intraprocessor communication

b) intraprocess and intraprocessor communication

c) <u>interprocess and interprocessor communication</u>

d) interprocessor communication

8. A multiprocessor operating system should perform

a) a mechanism to split a task into concurrent subtasks

b) optimize the system performance

c) handling structural or architectural changes

d) <u>all of the mentioned</u>

9. An operating system must possess

a) process-processor allocation strategies

b) mechanism to collect results of subtasks

c) software to improve overall performance

d) <u>all of the mentioned</u>

10. A multiprocessor operating system must take care of

a) authorized data access and data protection

b) <u>unauthorized data access and data protection</u>

c) authorized data access

d) data protection

Control Systems MCQ for Power System Engineering

1. Low power transducers called sensors prefer:

a) <u>Linear relationship between controlled variable and output variable</u>

b) Non-functional relationship between controlled variable and output variable

c) Non-linear relationship between controlled variable and output variable

d) Not related with each other

2. The chief advantage offered by the electronics is:

a) Differencing and stable amplification by Op-Amp

b) Stable amplification of power level by use of power transistor and SCR's

c) <u>Differencing and stable amplification of power level by Op-Amp</u>

d) No amplification with the Op-Amp

3. Which of the motions in actuators are preferred:

a) Translator

b)<u>Rotary</u>

c) Stationary

d) Non-Stationary

4. Assertion (A): Electric actuators are used control system for high torque applications.

Reason (R): Due to linear speed-Torque characteristics.

a) <u>Both A and R are true and R is correct explanation of A</u>

b) Both A and R are true but R is not correct explanation of A

c) A is true but R is false

d) A is false but R is true

5. Low power DC and AC motors are also known as __________

a) <u>Servomotors</u>

b) Tachogenerators

c) A.C. generators

d) D.C. generators

6.The torque developed by the motor when stationary with the full applied voltage__________

a) <u>Stalled torque</u>

b) Torque

c) Force

d) Couple

7. High torque/inertia ratio means:

a) Stalled torque

b) Stalled inertia

c) Stalled toque/inertia ratio

d) <u>Lower motor time constant</u>

9.DC motors can be modeled as:

a)Armature controlled

b)Field Controlled

c)<u>Both a and b</u>

d)None of the mentioned

10. Assertion (A): Pneumatic actuators are not as messy as hydraulic ones.

Reason (R): Pneumatic suffer from leakages and inherent inaccuracies.

a) Both A and R are true and R is correct explanation of A

b) <u>Both A and R are true but R is not correct explanation of A</u>

c) A is true but R is false

d) A is false but R is true

11. DC motors are constructed using:

a) <u>Permanent Magnet</u>

b) Electromagnet.

c) Magnets are not used

d) Plastics

12. Permanent magnets used for DC motors because of:

a) High residual flux density

b) High coercivity

c) <u>Both a and b</u>

d) Retentivity

13. A variable reluctance stepper motor is constructed of _______________ material with salient poles.

a) Paramagnetic

b) <u>Ferromagnetic</u>

c) Diamagnetic

d) Non-magnetic

14. In a three-stack 12/8-pole VR motor, the rotor pole pitch is

a) 15º

b) 30º

c) <u>45º</u>

d) 60º

15. A stepper motor having a resolution of 300 steps/rev and running at 2400 rpm has a pulse rate of- pps.

a) 4000

b) 8000

c) <u>6000</u>

d) 10,000

16. If a hybrid stepper motor has a rotor pitch of $36°$ and a step angle of $9°$, the number of its phases must be

a) <u>4</u>

b) 2

c) 3

d) 6

17. The rotor of a stepper motor has no

a) Windings

b) Commutator

c) Brushes

d) <u>All of the mentioned</u>

18. A stepping motor is a ______________ device.

a) Mechanical

b) Electrical

c) Analogue

d) <u>Incremental</u>

19. The rotational speed of a given stepper motor is determined solely by the

a) Shaft load

b) <u>Step pulse frequency</u>

c) Polarity of stator current

d) Magnitude of stator current.

20. Which of the following phase switching sequence represents half-step operation of a VR stepper motor ?

a) A, B, C,A........

b) A, C, B,A.......

c) AB, BC, CA, AB........

d) <u>A, AB, B, BC........</u>

21. A stepper motor may be considered as a ______________ converter.

a) Dc to dc

b) Ac to ac

c) Dc to ac

d) <u>Digital-to-analogue</u>

22. What is the step angle of a permanent-magnet stepper motor having 8 stator poles and 4 rotor poles?

a) 60º

b) 45º

c) 30º

d) 15º

www.ingramcontent.com/pod-product-compliance
Lightning Source LLC
Chambersburg PA
CBHW050800160726
48004CB00002B/642